ESPRESSO!

DRINKS, DESSERTS AND MORE

SHEA STURDIVANT & STEVE TERRACIN

THE CROSSING PRESS, FREEDOM, CA 95019

To Pop, who started it all.

Library of Congress Cataloging-in-Publication Data
Sturdivant, Shea.
 Espresso! : drinks, desserts, and sauces / by Shea Sturdivant &
Steve Terracin
   p. cm.
 ISBN 0-89594-514-2 (cloth). — ISBN 0-89594-513-4 (paper)
 1. Cookery (coffee) 2. Espresso. I. Terracin, Steve. II. Title.
TX819.C6S78   1991
641.6'373—dc20   91-24747
                                                       CIP

Acknowledgments

In the course of living your life, if you're real lucky, you meet people who influence you in a positive way. We've both been blessed by knowing quite a few of these people and want to thank them for being a part of our lives.

Thanks to Bob Sturdivant, Shea's brother. He made her "coffee milk" when she was a little girl and got her hooked on coffee at a young age. When they started a coffee business, he stayed behind the scenes, roasted the coffee, and gave her support and encouragement.

Thanks to Grant and Kathy Heath who made Shea her very first espresso and never lost their sense of humor or interest as we both talked endlessly to them about espresso.

Thanks to Dennis Hayes and David Copeland for their encouragement and support through the many months of this project. They moved *Espresso!* from idea to conclusion.

Thanks to William F. Rellstab for being "Mr. R.," friend, confidant, literary critic and very special to us.

And to Teri Hope, Abby Nash, Jim Tarantino, Richard Donnelly, and Susan Friedman for their contributions of recipes and editing that helped move this text from a rough draft to a finished book,

Most of all, we want to thank our readers and acknowledge you for the journey you are about to undertake.

Contents

Introduction

❖◆❖

Before we begin our discussion, brew a cup of french roast (better yet, have someone do it for you). Settle into your favorite chair, and venture with us into the world of espresso, a world thought by many to be the finest possible expression of a coffee bean.

The word espresso is from an Italian word meaning fast. It has the same lineage as the American word express, so it is little wonder that espresso was Americanized to expresso.

When properly prepared with quality ingredients, espresso is a rich, full-bodied drink with a distinctive flavor and aroma that hints at chocolate. Because espresso delivers such a burst of intense coffee flavor, first-time sippers usually either love it or hate it. Rarely is the response noncommittal. Espresso is potent for many reasons, one being the large amount of coffee used. You need as many beans to make 4 ounces of espresso as you need for 2 cups of brewed coffee. No cup of brewed coffee, regardless of how strong you make it, can come close to duplicating espresso. If you take a sip of brewed coffee then sip espresso, you will find espresso has a much richer flavor, much as heavy cream tastes richer than skim milk.

Although espresso is rich in flavor, it is relatively low in caffeine. A standard 2 ounce cup of espresso typically contains 45 mg. of caffeine compared to 75 mg. in an 8 ounce cup of brewed coffee. Caffeine content is determined by the coffee beans and the length of time water is in contact with the ground coffee. The pressurized extraction of espresso is accomplished in a few seconds of water contact. In a typical coffee brewing cycle, water contact is between three and five minutes.

How Espresso Is Made

Espresso is made by quickly forcing hot water and steam through finely ground and firmly compressed coffee bean granules. The principle has been around for hundreds of years in the form of the two-tiered moka pot. A moka pot requires more attention than an automatic machine but it will work anywhere there is sufficient heat. The moka pot will be used to explain espresso extraction. We will then explore the evolution of refinements that led to modern sophisticated machines developed by Gaggia and Valente.

Moka Pot

A moka pot has three basic components: bottom steam chamber, granule basket, and upper reservoir with a central pedestal having two opposing holes in its sides at the very top. You begin making espresso by filling the steam chamber with water. Grind the beans and pack the granules into the funnel-shaped basket. Grinding and its implications will be discussed later. The best pack is achieved by tamping granules in even layers, much like a pipe smoker tamps tobacco into a pipe. Tamp several layers of granules into the basket.

After firmly packing the basket, place it into the steam chamber then screw the steam chamber onto the upper reservoir so there is a snug fit against the rubber seal. Make sure to run your finger along the rubber seal to remove any loose granules. Place the pot on the stove and turn the heat to high. Leave the lid off the top chamber so that you can observe what's happening. Inside the steam chamber, water heats and steam collects. As steam builds, it forces down on the surface of the hot water and causes water to travel up the basket tube through the packed granules, and a thick, frothy brown liquid flows into the upper reservoir. Immediately remove the pot from the stove top. If steam gets too hot,

Moka Pot

espresso burns. Shortly after removing the pot from the heat, the flow of espresso slows. Through judicious application and removal of heat, you will be able to produce an even flow of water and steam from the bottom chamber, through the granules, and into the upper reservoir.

When water reaches its boiling point in a confined space like the moka pot steam chamber, it absorbs massive amounts of heat without increasing in temperature. Damp steam is formed and extra heat energy is stored in steam. When more heat is applied the heat of steam increases further. After pressure builds high enough to overcome resistance provided by packed coffee granules, hot water and steam pass through the granules. If steam is too hot, the granules burn. You must be very attentive to maintain steam and the pressure it provides in the lower chamber without overheating it. You want to maintain an even flow from the top of the reservoir pedestal without causing an eruption. Attention, patience, and a little practice is all it takes.

Clean equipment will make a world of difference in the taste of espresso. Unclean equipment will cause your espresso to have a musty taste from spoiled coffee solids remaining in the pot. Clean your equipment in a solution of vinegar and baking soda.

Espresso Machine

The espresso machine was developed in an attempt to gain control over temperature and pressure elements of espresso extraction. The first machines appeared at the end of the 19th century. They were simply bigger, flashier versions of the moka with an impressive array of gauges and spigots.

An alternative machine that quickly made espresso in volume was needed. This need was addressed in 1843 by Edward Loysel de Santais who applied principles developed in 1822 by Louis Bernard Rabaut. After twelve years of development, Loysel de Santais's machine was exhibited in 1865 at the Paris Exposition and produced large quantities of an espresso-like beverage.

Luigi Bezzera was the first commercial manufacturer of espresso machinery. His invention, a precursor of modern espresso machines, was introduced in Milan in 1906 at the first meeting of what was to become Italy's most prestigious trade fair, Fiera Campionara. Bezzera's invention could produce unlimited amounts of espresso because of its vertical boiler. Unfortunately, he spent all of his money inventing the machine and had to sell his patent.

Disderio Pavoni bought rights to Bezzera's machine and began mass production in 1910. Over the next few decades, these large, steam-driven behemoths continued to evolve. In these old machines, steam pressure was regulated by a "barista," a person who tended the espresso bar. The resulting beverage was bitter or sweet depending largely on the artistry of the barista. In 1935, Francesco Illy substituted compressed air for steam and produced the first automatic machine.

In 1945, consistency of espresso was greatly improved when Achilles Gaggia introduced the modern espresso machine. Gaggia used a mechanical piston to replace steam pressure. In Gaggia's machine, a lever on a heavy spring is pulled down to allow hot water into a piston chamber through a port in the bottom of the chamber. When the lever is released, the rising piston seals the bottom port and very quickly pressurizes water, forcing it through the coffee granules with haste. This fast, high pressure extraction of espresso produces a thick layer of foam, or crema, signature of good espresso. At the end of the decade, Ernesto Valente, who produced the Faema espresso machine, replaced the spring in Gaggia's lever machine with a rotating pump powered by a small electric motor.

Until the appearance of Gaggia's machine, espresso was easily burned. Modern machines allow for independent control of temperature and pressure, thereby improving chances for increased quality and consistency of espresso.

Commercial Espresso Maker

Coffee Bean—Star of the Show

The history of coffee is steeped in myth and legend. Scientific evidence suggests that coffee was crushed and mixed with fat and eaten by tribes on high central plains of Ethiopia. Africans later fermented ripe coffee fruit into wine. Coffee was probably first boiled and used as a hot drink about 675 A.D. in Arabia near the Red Sea. Coffee remained shrouded in mystery as a medicine and as a religious ceremonial drink for hundreds of years until it became popular as a drink in Near Eastern public coffee houses. Several times governments tried to prohibit public consumption of coffee. Because prohibition proved unworkable, restrictions were lifted and profits from coffee taxation rationalized its legality.

Coffee remained a closely guarded commodity among the Arab nations. For centuries cultivators allowed only boiled beans to be exported from the port of Mocha in Yemen. This was to prevent competition that would result if fertile beans were planted and cultivated elsewhere. During the 17th century, legend tells of coffee seeds that were spirited off to India and then to the Dutch East Indian island of Java where successful, large scale cultivation was established. Java remains as a popular synonym for coffee and Mocha-Java is a blend of the two oldest strains of coffee beans. In 1714, through an adventure that could fill a Michener tale, the French succeeded in establishing a coffee tree on the West Indian island of Martinique from an imported live cutting. That single cutting is the ancestor of all trees on all plantations in the West Indies and in Central and South America. Now the Americas produce about two-thirds of the world supply.

The coffee bean is actually a seed of the coffee cherry, the name for the fruit of the coffee tree. When ripe, the coffee cherry is an oblong, deep red fruit, a little smaller than the cherry that grew on George Washington's tree. Inside each cherry there are usually two seeds. Each seed is a coffee bean.

A small percentage of cherries are genetic mutations and contain only one seed known as a peaberry with a flavor and aroma different than their twin seeded sisters. You can buy peaberry coffee from some specialty roasting companies.

Of more than 30 species from genus Coffea in the Madder family, only two have commercial importance: C. arabica and C. canephora (robusta). Gourmet coffee is made only from species arabica. Coffee grows well in Arabia, India, Africa, on the islands of Java, Sumatra, Hawaii, West Indies, and in Central and South America.

Arabica coffee trees can grow to 30 feet high from rich, moist, well-drained soil at elevations up to tropical frost level of 6,000 feet. Cultivated trees are pruned to about five feet tall to promote heavy yields and to accommodate harvesting. When trees mature, at about five years, fragrant, white flowers bloom for only a few days. Fruit develops for six months following flowering, changing from light green through yellow and orange to deep crimson at harvest time. Average annual yield is five pounds of fresh fruit, enough to produce about one pound of dried coffee beans. As much as eight pounds of dried beans can be realized from a single tree with extensive fertilization and heavy pesticide spraying.

Coffee is harvested by handpicking fruit from clusters that grow on short stems. Workers travel through fields, collecting fruit in baskets attached to their belts, using tree hooks to pull down the tallest branches. Coffee trees often flower several times during a growing season and there is fruit in varying stages of development at first harvest. Workers must pick only red fruit and leave the green, yellow, and orange fruit for later harvest. Workers must go through fields several times to harvest an entire crop.

Pesticides

Organically grown coffee is gaining popularity due to extensive use of highly toxic pesticides used to improve coffee yields. If you decide to spend extra money for organic coffee, be sure that it is certified by the U.S. government. U.S. certification requires that soil be free from chemical application for many years prior to growing. Even though a grower doesn't spray pesticides, it doesn't assure that water washing over the fields is chemical free. Water from upper regions of a mountainside can bring chemicals. For this and other reasons, a U.S. certification requires an ongoing evaluation of fruit to assure chemical free growing conditions.

Coffee Mill

Following harvest, trucks usually transport coffee cherries to processing mills. At the mill, cherries are first sent to a pulper machine that removes the thick outer pulp and washes away the layer of mucilage that covers the parchment. Then the beans, still encased in parchment, are sent to mechanical dryers. Depending on the amount of beans, they are either completely dried in mechanical dryers, or partially dried mechanically and sent to vast drying floors used during peak harvest times. Some smaller mills use only drying floors. On drying floors, beans are periodically raked, much like you would rake a garden, to turn them and expose all surfaces. In either case, the drying process is complete when moisture content of beans is reduced to around 11%. After drying, parchment is brittle and beans are sent to hulling machines where parchment is easily removed. Beneath the parchment is a silver skin covering the beans. Sometimes beans are polished to remove the skin; otherwise beans are shipped with their skins intact and the skins end up in the bottom of coffee roasting machines

which must be cleaned regularly. Some roasters are willing to pay extra for polished beans so that the litter in the bottom of their roasting machines is reduced.

After hulling, beans are graded by size and weight. The largest beans are the premium bean size. The coffee industry believes the bigger the bean, the better the taste. Some roasters don't agree. Beans are further separated by weight on gravity tables, dual sloping tables that vibrate and bounce beans around. Heavier, premium beans move to the upper edge of the table and lighter, poorer quality beans, and twigs, rocks, and trash stay at the lower edge. As you might imagine, these vibrating tables and dancing beans make quite a racket. While beans travel the long table, workers remove debris from the beans and they are then funnelled into bags. After the sorting process, beans are sent to the polisher if necessary. From the coffee mill, beans are shipped to brokers throughout the world. Coffee brokerages in turn distribute to wholesale networks and then beans travel to local roasters. Decaffeination is available in very few locations (it's a patented process) and is usually commissioned by coffee brokers at the request of their customers.

Decaffeination

As with regular coffee, decaffeinated espresso has become commonplace. There are many ways coffee is decaffeinated. All use water or steam to open up the pores of the bean and draw the caffeine to the outer surface of the bean. However, from that point on, the methods vary.

In chemical decaffeination, a methylene chloride solvent is washed over the green coffee beans removing the caffeine. Steam is again applied, removing residual solvent. Chemical decaffeination

produces the most flavorful beans because the solvents are selective, removing caffeine but leaving the other solids that produce flavor. However, the amount of solvents remaining in the beans after roasting is debatable—some people argue that the heat necessary to roast the beans will drive out most of the methylene chloride, others have concerns that some of the solvent remains in the beans.

There is another chemical used for decaffeination, ethyl acetate (ethyl alcohol and vinegar). The process is similar to the above and may be safer than the hydrocarbon. In this method, when the beans are soaked in water, the caffeine leaches into the water. Ethyl acetate is added to the water and removes the caffeine. The water is then washed back over the beans. This is called the Natural Water Process.

There are two versions of true water decaffeination, both called Swiss Water Decaffeination. The first, in Switzerland, uses water to soak the beans. The water is then drawn off and filtered to remove the caffeine. To concentrate the flavor, the water is boiled down and then sprayed on the beans.

In the second Swiss Water Decaffeination, a later development of this method in Canada, the beans are discarded after the first soaking in water. New, premium beans are then soaked in the flavor-charged water from the first beans. This water pulls out the caffeine from the beans but leaves the flavor, because the flavor will not exit into the flavor-charged water.

There is one final method to decaffeinate coffee. The beans can be soaked in liquid carbon dioxide which removes the caffeine.

Good decaffeinated coffee should taste the same as caffeinated coffee, since caffeine has no taste. The primary considerations for the buyer should be taste and safety.

Roasting

To begin the roasting process, the roastmaster fires the roaster and preheats it to 400°F. The roastmaster selects the beans and loads them into the roaster. Color is a rough gauge that the roastmaster uses to determine when beans are approaching the correct roast level. Beans change color as they are roasted. The fat in the bean also dissolves into an oil that has no calories. Isn't it wonderful to know that you can drink coffee and get fats and oils without any calories?

As coffee beans tumble over heat in the roasting cylinder, the roastmaster periodically uses the tryer, a little sampling scoop, to check color. Once beans reach the proper color, the nose, eyes, and ears determine the exact moment to remove the beans from the fire. Each type of coffee bean has its own distinctive aroma that changes during roasting. Depending upon a complex set of growing condition variables including rainfall, sun, temperature, soil, elevation, and directional exposure, coffee will react differently to the 400°F temperature in the roasting oven. Experience is the only teacher that can educate the senses to subtle variations that signal "done." At that point, the roastmaster opens the oven door and spills the beans on to a cooling tray which has a set of rotating paddles that stir the beans while suction from below draws air through the beans down through holes in the bottom of the tray. Some roasting operations use a water spray to cool beans but water can deteriorate the flavor of coffee. If beans are not cooled rapidly, they will continue to roast from retained heat. The cooling tray stops the roasting process.

The coffee bean is chemically complex with some chemicals affecting taste and different chemicals affecting aroma. Solids that affect taste (including caffeine, trigonelline, chlorogenic acid, caffeic acids, amino acids, tannin, caffetannin, carbohydrates, and minerals) are minimally affected by roasting. Many aroma chemicals, known as volatiles, are produced by roasting. Important volatiles are organic acids, aldehydes, ketones, esters, amines, and mercaptans.

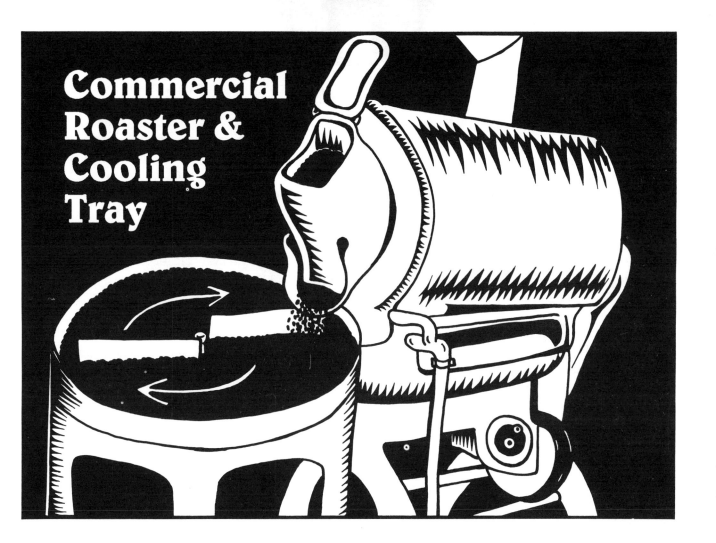

Commercial Roaster & Cooling Tray

Commercial coffees are generally roasted under the supervision of a roastmaster who oversees large scale, computer-controlled operations. Specialty coffees, however, are roasted in batches varying from a few pounds to several hundred pounds, under the direct control of a roastmaster experienced in "sight roasting" which calls on all of the senses to determine when the roast is completed. The roastmaster must be sensitive to the popping of the beans as they expand, the changing color, and the wafting coffee aroma. Some roasters go strictly by the aroma to determine the roast but most roastmasters use all of the senses. "Sight roasting" is not as financially efficient, but it provides a more finely controlled and better quality roast.

If you ever get the urge to roast your own coffee beans, resist it. You will probably burn or partially burn the beans and your activities will stink up the house for days. It's just not worth it! There are those who argue that it can be done at home with a Westbend Poppery II available for under $25. It's like a popcorn popper with a revolving paddle that keeps the beans turning so that they roast evenly. There are also home roasters available upwards of $100.

Levels of Roast

Roast definitions and preferences differ. Dark roasts are usually preferred for espresso. Within dark roasts, differences are so subtle that only a well-trained expert can detect them. Freshness is especially important for dark roasts. Because of regional variations, terminology will vary, but the following are pretty standard roast classifications:

Cinnamon—Light cinnamon brown. Has a pronounced nut-like flavor. Highest acidity level.
American—Even chestnut brown. Caramel-like flavor.

Full City—An in-between brown with a matte finish surface (no sheen). Fully developed coffee flavor with reduced acidity.

French—Dark brown with reddish brown highlights. The bean surface has a sheen (not to be confused with the oil that forms on the surface of all beans after a few days). Spicy taste and pungent aroma.

Italian—Very dark brown color with a glossy sheen. Pungent, robust aroma and flavor.

Selecting Fresh Beans

The following is a list of conditions with #1 providing the best flavor (in descending order):

1. Beans that have been roasted, then ground right out of the cooling tray, and immediately used to make coffee
2. Beans that have been roasted within the past few days, have been properly stored, and are ground just before making the coffee
3. Beans that are three or more days out of the roaster, have been properly stored, and are ground just before making the coffee
4. Prepackaged beans in an airtight bag that has a one-way carbon dioxide escape valve
5. Beans that are ground before you buy them
6. Commercially packaged, pre-ground, tins of coffee

As you can see from the list, freshness produces the best flavor. None of the other factors—blend, roast, grind, equipment—impact flavor and aroma in your cup of espresso as much as freshness.

As beans roast, oils that develop will migrate to the surface. As they cool, oils are absorbed back into the beans. Within three days, and usually sooner, oils will break to the surface again, releasing

carbon dioxide. Carbon dioxide is the natural ingredient that gives freshly roasted coffee its zip, much the same as carbon dioxide gives soda pop its zip. Grinding will speed release of carbon dioxide and the loss depletes flavor and aroma that characterize freshly roasted coffee.

When freshly roasted beans are stored in airtight containers, the carbon dioxide loss is slowed. Small one-way valves used in most of today's specialty packaging were developed in Milan, Italy by Goglio Luigi, SpA. These valves, known as "belly-button valves," allow freshly roasted coffee to be sealed immediately in an airtight bag. These valves allow carbon dioxide to escape from the bag, relieving built-up gas pressure. The valve also purges residual oxygen, thereby adding a few days of shelf life.

While bags protect beans from absorbing oxygen, they do nothing to retain carbon dioxide. This brings us full circle. If you want a fresh tasting cup of espresso, find a local roaster and hang out in the shop on roasting day.

When choosing a local roaster, follow these simple guidelines:

1. Find a shop that specializes in coffee beans.
2. Find a shop that roasts small batches every day.
3. When you enter the shop, it should be clean and smell like fresh coffee.
4. Beans should be in clean, airtight containers out of direct heat or sunlight.
5. Shop personnel should be knowledgeable about coffee, friendly, and approachable.
6. Brewed coffee should be available for sampling.
7. If the store sells flavored beans, there should be a separate grinder just for them.
8. Beans should be fresh. If you are unsure about the freshness of a bean, bite it. Fresh beans are brittle and will break apart in a burst of coffee flavor. Stale beans are rubbery and chewy.
9. And, of course, the shop should have a good espresso machine.

Espresso Beans

Beans for espresso are traditionally roasted dark, either French or Italian roast; however, different kinds of beans can be used. A word of caution here: some of the best coffees available make poor choices for espresso, notably Jamaican Blue Mountain and Kona. These fine lava soil grown beans do not respond well to espresso extraction. Save them for your coffee brew basket.

There are some beans that respond exceptionally well to the espresso extraction process. The following chart lists some of them, their flavor characteristics, and blending possibilities.

Brazil Santos—Full, strong, sweet taste. They provide a good base for blending. Can be used in proportions of 40% to 60%.

Celebes Kalossi—Medium bodied, rich flavor and aroma. Because of their winy acidity they are best used sparingly. Use 15% to 25%.

Costa Rican—Full bodied, mild flavor and fragrant. They provide a good base for blending. Can use 40% to 50%.

Colombian—Fine flavor and aroma with a distinct coffee liquor. They provide a good base for blending or use full strength. Blend at 40% to 50%.

Guatemalan—Mellow, rich, heavy flavor. A little goes a long way. Blend at 15% to 25%.

Kenyan—Full bodied, rich, smooth with a sharp taste. Blends well with beans that have a less pronounced taste. Use 15% to 25%.

Sumatran—Deep, heavy, syrupy flavor with good aroma and body. Use sparingly in amounts of 15% to 25%.

Storing Your Beans

Coffee beans grow stale in stages. First, aroma decreases as carbon dioxide leaves the bean. Then flavor decreases. Then rancidity develops. Dark roasted beans are particularly vulnerable to the third stage because of their high oil content. Decaffeinated beans are also very susceptible to spoilage.

For the ultimate in fresh espresso, buy small quantities from your local roaster every day or so. If this is not possible, make sure beans are fresh and buy whole beans.

Immediately transfer your beans to a freshly washed, dried, airtight container. Those glass jars with glass tops that have a trapeze-looking spring wire hinge arrangement pressing a rubber sealer washer between the jar and its top work very well. Keep your beans away from the heat and light. If you plan to use coffee within a few days, store it in the refrigerator. If you expect coffee to be around for more than a week, store it in the freezer.

When you take beans from the refrigerator or freezer, remove the beans you need and immediately return remaining beans to the cold. The longer they are in warm air, the more condensation will form on beans and this condensation will age beans faster.

After removing beans you need from cold storage, allow them to warm before grinding them.

Blending Beans

Most experts agree that the best cup of espresso is made with a blend of different bean types. However, there are many different espresso blends. Some insist that Robusta beans must be included, others say Arabica beans only. Different blends have unique flavors and in combination can enhance each other. Our recommendation is to experiment with a variety of blends to find the one that is right for you. You may find it helpful to keep notes on espresso blends.

Our blend preferences change frequently. Today our favorite is 75% dark roast Colombian Supremo mixed with 25% Kenya AA. We may stop in at our local roaster tomorrow and find they have a fresh roasted batch of Brazilian Santos and then we have to select what other beans will "co-star" in this new blend. Blending is not an exact science—experimentation is the key. Let your own taste buds guide the way.

Following are a few blending suggestions:

50% Brazilian Santos, 30% Kenyan or Tanzanian, and 20% Costa Rican
50% Costa Rican, 25% Colombian Supremo, and 25% Sumatran
50% Mexican, 25% Guatemalan, and 25% Kenyan
40% Brazilian Santos, 30% Kenyan, 15% Colombian Supremo, and 15% Costa Rican

Grinding Your Beans

Perfect espresso grind depends on several factors including your equipment, water temperature and pressure, and your taste preferences. No one can mandate taste preference. Some people prefer bitter, burned-tasting espresso. If you are one of them, you will not have a difficult time at all preparing espresso. Just grind your beans as fine as possible and use superheated water. Experts contend that good espresso should never be bitter and should never taste burned. These conditions are more difficult to achieve.

Grinders

Coffee bean grinders are available in two styles, unless we include mortar and pestle and then there are three. First, and most expensive, is the burr grinder which is an updated version of a millstone.

Burr grinders use two rotating, rough metal plates that tear beans apart as they are pressed and scraped against the plates. The second type of grinder is a blade grinder that is actually a miniature electric blender.

Burr grinders are available in two versions, manual and electric. Some people find satisfaction in grinding their coffee by hand—that is, until the morning they desperately want that first cup and have to spend five minutes grinding. Higher priced, electrically operated burr grinders are also available. Burr grinders often have settings that determine grind size. You will have to experiment with settings to obtain proper grind.

Electric blade grinders are less expensive, have a tendency to heat bean granules as the blade spins around inside, and have no grind settings. You can overcome heating problems by pressing the button for one second then releasing it for five seconds to let beans rest and cool before repeating the cycle. As far as grind settings go, you can experiment with the number of press and release cycles necessary to achieve proper grind. Regardless of the type of grinder you buy, look for a model with sloping sides. This reduces granule buildup and produces a more consistent grind.

The Grind

The amount of time granules are to be in contact with water determines the grind, or more specifically, size of coffee granules once they are ground. The longer granules are in contact with water, the larger granules should be, or coarser the grind. Percolated coffee has a long water contact time and the grind is coarse. Drip coffee has a shorter water contact time and uses a medium granule size or medium grind. Espresso granules barely have a chance to get wet as water and steam rush through. Espresso granules are finely ground. However, there is a limit to fine grinding. If granules are too fine, the espresso will be muddy and bitter.

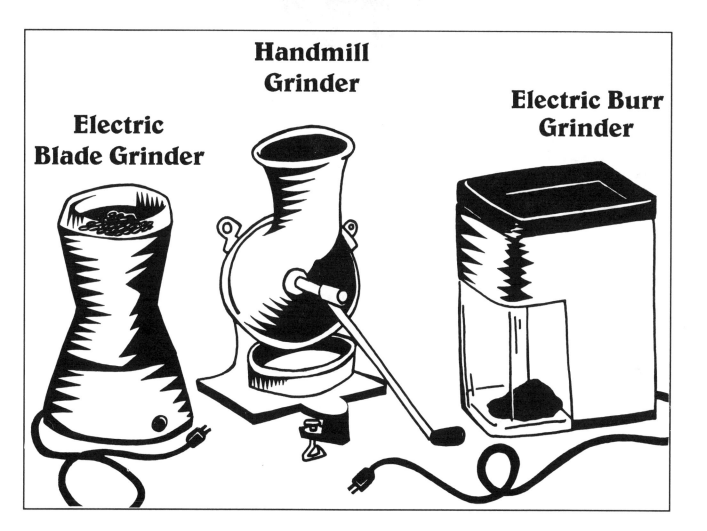

The best test for grind size is your own personal taste—if the espresso tastes perfect, the grind is probably just right. A good test for espresso grind is to rub the granules between your fingers. Granules should feel like fine sand. If they feel like powder, the grind is probably too fine. To test grind further after you prepare your espresso, dump the pod of spent granules from your basket and examine it. If the center of the pod is dry and crumbly and the taste of the espresso was weak and thin, the grind was too coarse. If the pod is wet and sloppy and the taste of the espresso was bitter, the grind was too fine. When coffee is ground too coarse, the water passes through too quickly and the spent pod looks dry and crumbly; not much coffee has been extracted. When coffee is ground too fine, the water backs up in the filter basket because it cannot get through the coffee powder easily. What water does get through overextracts and causes a bitter taste.

Home Espresso Machines

A moka pot is the manual, hands-on version of a home espresso machine. It won't generate the rich, foamy blanket of "crema" that covers a cup of espresso made in a machine with an electric pump, but it's inexpensive, serviceable, and you can take it with you on a backpacking trip. Moka pots are available for under $10 and range up to models with mirror-finished stainless steel and 24k gold accents costing considerably more.

Automatic machines with electric pumps force temperature-regulated water and steam through the coffee under independently controlled pressure. A basic model costs about $75. As the price increases, so do the bells and whistles. Many are equipped with a milk frother, some with a grinder.

Hydraulic-powered piston

Spring-powered piston

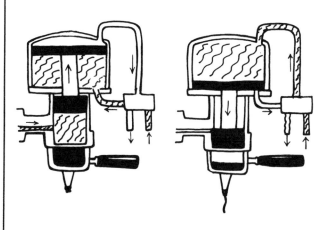

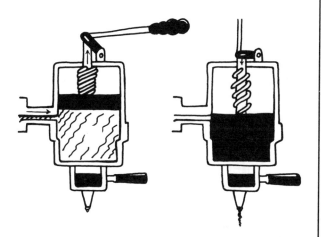

Tap water enters the main chamber, raising the large and small pistons, allowing heated water to enter the lower chamber. When the water in the main chamber is released, the pistons are driven downward by water released into the top chamber, forcing the heated water through the coffee grounds extracting the espresso. The lever raises the spring-controlled piston, allowing heated water into the lower chamber. When the piston is lowered, heated water is forced through the coffee grounds, extracting the espresso.

The automatic machines use the same basic principles as a moka pot and require the same attention to grind and tamping of granules. Once this preparation is finished, just follow the manufacturer's instructions for placing the granule basket into the machine and setting controls. Each machine is a bit different and you should read the manufacturer's instruction manual thoroughly to assure your safety, the well-being of your equipment, and the best possible cup of espresso.

Some side benefits of owning an automatic machine are probably not mentioned in your owner's manual. If your machine is equipped with a steam-powered milk frother, try frothing a raw egg in an 8 ounce coffee cup. Fluffy scrambled eggs anyone? Hot chocolate is divine when filled with frothy bubbles. Tea is dense and rich when steeped using the frother. Hot apple cider becomes a quick and easy drink.

Water for Your Espresso

A general rule for your espresso is to use only water that you would drink by the glass. The choices are spring water, tap water, filtered tap water, or distilled water. If you know your source, spring water is probably the best.

Frothing Milk

If the espresso machine you have or will buy does not have a milk frother, there is available one that sits on the stove. It is like a moka pot but has a nozzle. This costs about $40. Whole milk will taste better than nonfat milk.

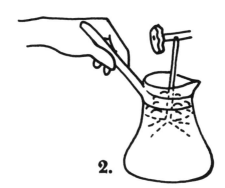

Steaming Milk

1. Inserting the steam jet and opening the valve.
2. Foaming the milk.

Good Espresso

As already stated, the quality of your cup of espresso is up to you. You are the one controlling grind and packing density, and water temperature, steam temperature and pressure. You are the one evaluating the final product.

Here are the important points to remember in making espresso:

Use freshly roasted beans.

If you must store beans, store them in an airtight container in the refrigerator or freezer.

Grind the coffee beans just before making espresso.

Keep your equipment clean.

Experiment with blends for variety and improved flavor.

Use water at 195°F if you can.

Use steam at 293°F if you can.

Espresso Terms

Acidity—Not the same as an acid stomach. Some acidity in coffee is desirable. Acidity in this case means smooth and rich with a distinct snap to the taste.

Arabica—A species of coffee used in the gourmet trade. Grown at high altitudes, with distinct taste characteristics that vary depending on the country of origin, soil it is grown in, and processing methods used.

Aroma—A desirable characteristic. The aroma of freshly ground and brewed coffee has been known to bring the dead back to life in the morning. Varies according to the country of origin. More distinct in coffees of the arabica species.

Blending—Combining beans with different characteristics to achieve a well-rounded taste and aroma. Beans of different roasts are also blended according to personal taste preferences.

Body—When associated with coffee, it means sense of heaviness or richness, rather than taste.

Break—Term associated with coffee roasting. It is used to describe coffee oils breaking to the surface.

Brown Gold—Term used by Andres Uribe to describe coffee. He also authored a book of the same name.

Cappuccino—A type of coffee beverage made with approximately one-third espresso, one-third hot milk, topped with one-third foam (not whipped cream).

Crema—A dense foam that tops espresso. The freshness of the coffee, its origin, grind, and equipment used determine if crema will be present.

Espresso—A concentrated coffee beverage, extracted under pressure, with heavy body and a distinct aroma. Traditionally imbibed in small amounts and served in a demitasse cup.

Espresso System—A set of factors influencing the final cup of espresso. The system is comprised of the blend of bean, the roast, the storage of the beans, the grind, the espresso machine, and the active participation of the person preparing the espresso to adjust any components of the system as needed.

Expresso—An incorrect way to spell and say espresso, used by the uninitiated rather than the devotee.

Moka—A stove-top coffee maker that makes an espresso style of coffee beverage. Precursor of the modern espresso machine.

Overextraction—When too much coffee is extracted during the brewing process. This results in a bitter, strong taste. Can happen if the grind is too fine for the brewing method or if the water is too hot. It can also happen when the water pressure is too high or the coffee is too tightly packed.

Pyrolysis—A series of chemical changes occurring in coffee beans during the roasting process. As a result, the substances responsible for coffee's aroma and flavor are released.

Quaker—A shriveled, underdeveloped coffee bean. Tends to roast a little lighter than other beans. The taste of the bean is not effected.

Recovery Time—The length of time it takes an espresso machine to recover from making one espresso until it is ready to make another.

Roast—A controlled application of heat that causes physical and chemical changes in coffee beans.

Robusta—A species of coffee bean that is not used in the gourmet trade, but is used in some commercial blends. Grown at lower elevations than arabica and not as susceptible to disease. It has body, but not much taste or aroma.

Sight Roast—A method of roasting that uses the senses of the roaster to determine roast temperature and length.

Solvent—A liquid in which a substance can be dissolved. In the coffee trade, the term is most often used to describe something that dissolves caffeine in green coffee beans.

Stinker—An overfermented coffee bean. Can be identified by its discolored appearance and bad smell. Cannot be easily detected in green coffee.

Swiss Water Process—A type of decaffeination process that extracts caffeine from coffee beans using water as a solvent. The caffeine is removed from the water by carbon filters and then the water is washed back over the beans so the flavor components can rejoin the beans.

Tipping—The charring of the ends of the coffee beans by roasting at too high a temperature too quickly.

Tryer—A long narrow scoop used by roasters to pull beans out of the roaster during the roasting process. Especially useful during "sight roasting," as the roasters must "try" the beans during the roast to determine when they are properly roasted.

Underextraction—When too little coffee is extracted during the brewing process. This can happen when not enough coffee is used, the coffee is too coarsely ground, or the water temperature is too cool. In the case of espresso extraction, this can also occur when the water pressure is too low or the coffee is too loosely packed.

1
Hot Drinks

Now that you've mastered the fundamentals, it's time to reap the benefits. Head for the kitchen and "espresso" yourself!

Steaming the Milk

Our drink recipes use only whole milk because it contains more butterfat and steams easier than a low-fat milk. It also provides a good froth for cappuccino and the correct "head" of hot milk needed for latte drinks. However, extra-rich or low-fat milk can be substituted.

Your well-stocked espresso kitchen should have a steaming pitcher with a handle, fluted lip, and a wide bottom. Most espresso machines now include a steaming pitcher and a tamper. Steaming is tricky. It takes patience and plenty of practice. Keep the steam tip near the surface of the milk and lower the pitcher as the froth rises. This allows the steam to drive the milk down, heating it evenly. Use your wrist to gently move the milk level up and down. This permits you to control the consistency of the froth/steam. When preparing more than one cappuccino, add milk for each steaming.

Serving Espresso

Demitasse cups and saucers are typically used for traditional espresso drinks. Tall glasses (10 to 12 ounces) are used for cold espresso drinks with juices and alcohol. Glass mugs (10 to 12 ounces) with handles are preferable for hot espresso drinks. Remember to place a tall spoon in the glass mugs prior to pouring hot coffee, to prevent possible cracking.

In America, espresso is generally served in a pre-warmed cup and saucer. We prefer stoneware demitasse cups because they retain heat longer and also insulate your hand.

For decorative purposes, place the teaspoon on the saucer with a little zest of lemon on the mouth of the spoon. Try dunking and quickly removing the lemon. Or put a twist of lemon rind on the saucer edge. Other garnish suggestions are listed throughout the recipe section of this book.

Espresso usually contains 6 to 7 grams of coffee per serving (approximately 2 to 3 ounces). Always use fresh cold water. Please note that all espresso recipes may be made with caffeinated or decaffeinated coffee.

Cappuccino

An Italian tradition, the simplest espresso drink recipe is this one for cappuccino. If you want the real thing, be sure to use whole or extra-rich milk for a rich, creamy consistency.

1/4 cup (2 ounces) brewed espresso, hot
3/4 cup (6 ounces) whole milk, frothed/
  steamed
Dash cinnamon or nutmeg

Prepare the espresso and froth/steam the cold whole milk. Remember to keep the steam diffuser tip near the top of the milk while you move the container up and down. This will heat the milk faster, give you more control, and avoid messy blow-outs. Once the milk has been frothed gently, place the fluff carefully into the cup of espresso to a point above the lip of the cup. Sprinkle with cinnamon or your favorite spice. Serve hot.

Serves one.

Cafe Mocha

❖◆❖

This is the chocolate drink for chocoholics. If you like the taste of chocolate more than the taste of coffee, you'll really love it. You can use low-fat milk here; however, it won't have the same thick consistency and will be lighter in flavor. You can use any kind of good chocolate to shave over the top of the drink. White chocolate adds a nice decorative touch and good flavor.

1/4 cup (2 ounces) brewed espresso, hot
1 cup (8 ounces) whole milk
3 teaspoons chocolate syrup or dry chocolate milk blend (adjust to your personal preference)
Dash cocoa powder or shaved chocolate

Prepare the espresso and set aside. Mix the chocolate syrup and milk then froth/steam the mixture. The chocolate milk does not need to be as frothed as it is when you prepare Cappuccino. Place a long-handled spoon into a tall glass mug (10 to 12 ounces); this will help keep the glass from breaking when you add the espresso and hot chocolate milk. Next add the hot chocolate milk, leaving space at the top of the mug for the espresso. Gently pour the espresso through the hot chocolate milk and top with any remaining chocolate milk. Serve with sprinkles of cocoa powder or shaved chocolate.

Serves one.

Cafe Au Chocolat

We've learned to keep the chocoholics at bay with this sophisticated after-dinner drink. It's no fuss. A great substitute for a gooey dessert.

1/2 cup (4 ounces) brewed espresso, hot
1/4 cup (2 ounces) whole milk
2 teaspoons chocolate milk powder
Pinch orange rind
Cinnamon and/or nutmeg, to taste
Whipped cream

Combine first four ingredients and steam. Pour into a 8 to 10 ounce mug, top with whipped cream, and dust with cinnamon and/or nutmeg.

Serves one.

Cafe Latte

❖◆◆

We like to think of a latte as a reverse cappuccino. It's a pleasing option for people who like hot milk more than they like espresso.

1 cup (8 ounces) steamed whole milk
1/4 cup (2 ounces) brewed espresso, hot
Pinch nutmeg

Froth milk and pour into a 10 ounce mug (preferably clear) and very slowly pour espresso down the inner edge of the mug. You should get a layered effect with liquid milk on the bottom, coffee in the middle and a generous amount of foam on top. Serve hot.

Serves one.

Hawaiian Espresso

❖◆◆

Sometimes we feel like coconut, sometimes we don't...but when we do, this is our espresso drink. Some coconut lovers will prefer the rich taste of the cream of coconut concentrate (especially the brand Coco Lopez), but others will select the thinner taste of coconut milk.

1/2 cup (4 ounces) brewed espresso, hot
1/4 cup (2 ounces) whole milk
1 1/2 tablespoons cream of coconut or
  coconut milk

Make a single espresso. Combine the milk and the cream of coconut concentrate or coconut milk into a pot and steam. Add the espresso, shake or stir and pour into a mug.

Serves one.

Espresso Mandarino

We use bottled orange syrup here, the kind that is used to make orangeade with tap water or soda water. The combination of the coffee and orange is outstanding.

1/4 cup (2 ounces) brewed espresso, hot
1 to 2 tablespoons orange syrup, to taste
Orange slice

Make a single espresso. Add the orange syrup and garnish with orange slice.

Serves one.

Espresso Spiced Apple

We bring this out for Halloween. It's surprising what fruit juices, in this case apple juice, does for the espresso.

1 cup (8 ounces) brewed espresso, hot
2 tablespoons cinnamon
2 tablespoons nutmeg
3/4 cup (6 ounces) apple juice

Add the cinnamon, nutmeg, and apple juice to the hot espresso. Heat the mixture and serve hot.

Serves one.

Honey Espresso

This is a quick and easy way to get an energy boost when we feel those late afternoon doldrums. It's also nice as a non-alcoholic holiday toddy.

1 cup (8 ounces) brewed espresso, hot
2 teaspoons honey, adjusted to taste
Whipped cream
Cinnamon
Nutmeg

Make espresso and pour half in each of two tall glasses. Add 1 teaspoon of honey to each glass and taste to see if more is needed. Top with whipped cream and dust with cinnamon and nutmeg. Serve hot.

Serves two.

Minty Lemon Espresso

1 lemon, rind and peel
1 cup (8 ounces) brewed espresso, hot
2 tablespoons honey
3 teaspoons mint leaves

Grate the rind of one lemon into a pot containing espresso. Add the lemon juice and honey. Taste and add more honey if necessary. Add the mint leaves. Stir, then strain the mixture through cheesecloth and serve hot.

Serves two.

Cafe Maria Espresso

◆◆◆

We're particularly fond of this recipe. We like to think that it calms our souls and, as a bonus, the internal rumbling from a spicy meal.

3/4 cup (6 ounces) brewed espresso, hot
3/4 cup (6 ounces) chocolate milk
1/4 cup (2 ounces) Tia Maria
Whipped cream
Cinnamon

Mix the espresso, chocolate milk, and Tia Maria in a steaming pitcher and steam just to heat evenly, not to froth or whip. Pour mixture into two coffee mugs and add the whipped cream and dust with cinnamon. Serve hot.

Serves two.

Flaming Espresso

❖◆❖

If you want to impress someone, this one's for you. It complements a heavy meal. Sipped slowly and luxuriously, it soothes and awakens all the senses.

2 cups (16 ounces) brewed espresso, hot
1/2 cup (4 ounces) dark rum
1/2 cup (4 ounces) Cointreau
Zest of 1 orange, grated
6 cloves

Brew the espresso. Set aside. Combine the dark rum, Cointreau, grated orange rind and cloves in a bowl. Standing at the table use a long match to set the liquid on fire. Let the flame burn out. Then add the espresso, which has cooled somewhat. Pour into 4 tall glasses. By the way, if anyone asks, by flaming the spirits, you burn off almost all of the alcohol. Serve hot.

Serves four.

Espresso a l'Orange

This tasty drink will have you thinking warm, tropical thoughts in no time. It makes for perfect dessert by itself.

2 oranges
2/3 cup whipping cream
2/3 cup confectioner's sugar
2 tablespoons butter, melted
1/4 cup white granulated sugar
1/2 cup (4 ounces) brandy
1/4 cup (2 ounces) Grand Marnier (or any orange liqueur)
1 1/2 cups (12 ounces) brewed espresso, hot

Cut 4 pieces of zest from the orange peel to use as garnish. Juice the oranges. Whip the cream and confectioner's sugar and chill. Place the sugar and butter in a saucepan over low heat until the sugar dissolves, and add the orange juice, brandy, and Grand Marnier. Ignite and let burn for 30 seconds. (If you feel a little nervous about this technique, turn the heat up and let the liquid almost come to a boil, then remove from the heat.) Have the espresso prepared and, while still hot, pour into 4 mugs. Divide the orange blend evenly. Top with the whipped cream and garnish with orange zest.

Serves four.

Espresso Bustamante

This is the ultimate drink for viewing someone's etchings.

1/4 cup (2 ounces) Cognac
1/4 cup (2 ounces) Kahlua
1/8 cup (1 ounce) Benedictine
7/8 cup (7 ounces) brewed espresso, hot
Unsweetened whipped cream
1/8 cup (1 ounce) Tia Maria
Grated white chocolate, optional

In warmed, heatproofed 12 ounce mug or glass, combine the Cognac, Kahlua, and Benedictine. Pour in hot espresso. Top with whipped cream, drizzle Tia Maria on top, and sprinkle with grated white chocolate, if desired. Serve hot.

Serves two.

Irish Espresso

❖◆❖

We both like this after a long Fall walk...it must be the Irish in us.

1/4 cup (2 ounces) Irish whiskey
   (preferably Jameson's)
1 1/4 cups (10 ounces) brewed espresso,
   hot
Sugar, to taste
Cream, to taste

In a tall glass, mix the whiskey, espresso, and sugar. Pour the cream over a spoon into the coffee and drink the warm liquid through the cool layer of cream.

Serves two.

Cafe Brulot Espresso

◆◆

There is a legend, handed down through generations of Louisiana folk, that Jean Lafitte, the pirate, warmed himself by mixing what he had aboard his brig—coffee, brandies, spices, and citrus. The bone chilling cold of the Louisiana swamps in winter gave birth to his liquid legacy.

1 4-inch cinnamon stick
8 to 10 whole cloves
Zest of 2 oranges, in thin slivers
Zest of 2 lemons, in thin slivers
6 lumps sugar
1 cup (8 ounces) brandy, warmed
1/2 cup (4 ounces) Curacao, warmed
1/2 cup (4 ounces) Cointreau
2 cups (16 ounces) brewed espresso, hot
Lemon juice and sugar, optional

Combine spices, peels and sugar in a pan; mash with the ladle and add brandy, Curacao and Cointreau. Stir, ignite with a long match, and ladle flaming spirits back and forth from the pan to another bowl, creating the effect of a column of fire. When the sugar has dissolved, gradually add the brewed espresso, stirring until the flame burns out. Strain into 8-ounce cups that may be ringed with lemon and sugar. Serve hot.

Serves four.

Espresso Cherry Flip

◆◆

The combination of flavors here is marvelous—the cherry, the chocolate, the espresso. How to live well!

1/8 cup (1 ounce) cherry-flavored brandy
2 tablespoons (1/2 ounce) Creme de
   Cacao
1 cup (8 ounces) brewed espresso, hot
Whipped cream
Cherry with stem

Pour brandy and liqueur into 2 pre-warmed mugs. Add hot espresso, approximately 4 ounces each. Top with a mound of whipped cream and garnish with cherry. Serve hot.

Serves two.

Espresso Royale

❖◆❖

This is a simple, true recipe. Many people prefer the straightforward merging of cognac with espresso.

1/2 cup (4 ounces) brandy/cognac
4 sugar cubes
1/2 cup (4 ounces) brewed espresso, hot

Place a sugar cube in each of 4 demitasse cups. Fill cups half full of brewed espresso. Slowly add brandy to fill the cup (if done correctly, brandy will rise to the top). Ignite brandy; let burn a few seconds and stir well. Try brown sugar cubes for a change of taste.

Serves two.

2
Cold Drinks

Timothy's Iced Cappuccino

Toronto is blessed with many excellent coffee shops, including Timothy's on Yonge St. You'll have to ask the manager to make this drink specially for you as it's not on the menu. A perfect cooler for a hot summer day.

1/2 cup (4 ounces) brewed espresso, at
  room temperature
6 to 8 ice cubes
1/2 cup (4 ounces) whole milk
2 tablespoons honey
Whipped cream
Chocolate shavings

Blend the espresso, ice cubes, milk and honey in a blender until liquified. Pour into a tall glass and top with whipped cream and chocolate shavings. You can use skim milk but there is marked difference in the taste.

Serves one.

Iced Cafe Au Lait

❖◆❖

One blistering hot afternoon we came up with a brand new thirst quencher, espresso ice cubes! Pour espresso into trays, then freeze. Leftover espresso will never be wasted with this method. Add these cubes to your favorite espresso drink recipes.

1/2 cup (4 ounces) whole milk
1/2 teaspoon sugar
4 frozen espresso cubes
1/4 cup (2 ounces) iced espresso

In a blender, combine (in order) the first three ingredients. Blend until espresso cubes/balls are crushed. Pour into a tall glass or mug and add the strained iced espresso down the side of the glass.

Serves one.

Cold Mocha Espresso

❖◆❖

1 teaspoon good quality cocoa (heaping)
1 or 2 teaspoons brown sugar, to taste
1/4 teaspoon vanilla extract
1 cup (8 ounces) milk
1/4 cup (2 ounces) brewed espresso, at
   room temperature

Heat first four ingredients and stir gently. Bring to a near boil and remove from the heat. Let cool. Add 1/3 cup of this mixture to espresso and pour over ice cubes.

This mixture minus the espresso may be made in quantity and chilled in the refrigerator.

Always use 1/3 cup mocha mixture to 1/4 cup espresso.

Top with hot frothed milk and sprinkle with cocoa powder. This looks best served in a tall glass.

Serves one.

Frosty Espresso

We have found this to be an excellent dessert drink, especially after fish.

1/4 cup sugar
2 cups (16 ounces) brewed espresso, hot
1/2 teaspoon almond extract

Dissolve sugar in the espresso while still hot. Let cool. Add almond extract, and pour mixture into metal tray or bowl. Freeze until almost hard. Beat well, and freeze again to sherbet consistency. Turn into sherbet glasses; top with whipped cream and a cherry.

Serves four.

Espresso Ice Cream Soda

1 1/2 cups (12 ounces) brewed espresso, at
  room temperature
1/2 cup light corn syrup
1/2 cup light cream
1 pint coffee ice cream
Sparkling water

Combine espresso, syrup, and cream. Mix well. Divide among 4 tall glasses. Add a scoop of ice cream to each glass and fill with ice cold sparkling water.

Serves four.

Espresso Nectar

❖❖❖

1 1/2 cups (12 ounces) brewed espresso, refrigerated
1 pint coffee ice cream
1 tablespoon Angostura Bitters

Place all ingredients in a blender and whirl until smooth and cream. Pour into tall glasses.

Serves three or four.

Espresso Mandarino

This is luxuriously rich, just grab a tall glass and find a partner. Good for breakfast or brunch.

1/2 cup (4 ounces) brewed espresso, refrigerated
4 mandarin orange slices, canned
1/4 cup (2 ounces) half-and-half
2 large scoops vanilla ice cream, divided
Cinnamon and/or nutmeg, to taste

Combine the espresso, orange slices, half-and-half, and 1 large scoop of ice cream in a blender and whirl. Divide into 2 tall iced glasses. Top each glass with a half scoop of ice cream. Sprinkle with cinnamon and/or nutmeg. Serve with straws.

Serves two.

Espresso Eggnog Punch

❖◆

The perfect holiday punch for the whole family.

1 1/2 cups sugar
3 cups boiling water
2 cups (16 ounces) brewed espresso, hot
10 egg yolks
2 1/2 quarts whole milk
10 egg whites

Add sugar to boiling water and stir until dissolved. Let come to a boil and then remove from heat. Add espresso. Stir well, cover, and let stand for 15 minutes. Let drip through two thicknesses of wet cheesecloth which has been placed in a strainer (or a #6 paper filter) and cool. Beat egg whites until stiff and set aside. Beat egg yolks, stir in coffee mixture slowly. Add milk, blend well, and fold in the egg whites. If a smooth instead of fluffy eggnog is desired, the egg yolks and whites may be beaten together. Pour in a punch bowl and sprinkle with nutmeg. Serve in punch cups.

Serves thirty to thirty-five.

Mocha Yogurt

❖◆❖

For a luxurious weekend brunch or after dinner, this cold and creamy espresso drink tastes like a decadent dessert. After concocting many variations, we decided that we like the Kahlua best. You be the judge—choose any chocolate or coffee liqueur you like.

8 ounces plain or vanilla yogurt
1 cup (8 ounces) brewed espresso, refrigerated
1 tablespoon grated or shaved semisweet chocolate
1/4 cup (2 ounces) Kahlua or Creme de Cacao
Ice cubes
6 chocolate-covered coffee beans (optional)

Mix all of the ingredients (except for the chocolate-covered coffee beans) in a blender, adding a small amount of ice to taste. Blend until the mixture is creamy like a milk shake. Now pour the mixture into 2 tall glasses. Decorate with the shaved sweet chocolate and the chocolate-covered coffee beans...3 to a glass. Superstition and coffee lore say that it is bad luck to put an even number of coffee beans in any coffee drink. Serve with a straw.

Serves two.

Espresso Cola Fizz

This summer cooler is just what the doctor ordered for a hot day in the shade. We think this drink tastes best in the late afternoon or early evening. Don't worry if you have only one type of rum—the recipe still comes out great. Wear white and "think cool."

1/4 cup (2 ounces) light rum
1/4 cup (2 ounces) dark rum
1 cup (8 ounces) brewed espresso,
   refrigerated
1 1/2 cups (12 ounces) cola
2 tablespoons lemon juice
Crushed ice

Pour all the ingredients in a blender or shaker and mix well. Pour the mixture over the crushed ice in 2 tall glasses. Serve with straws.

Serves two.

Espresso Tropicana

Add a little ice cream and this could be an espresso rum soda.

1 cup (8 ounces) brewed espresso, refrigerated
1/2 cup (4 ounces) dark rum
1 cup (8 ounces) light cream
Sparkling water
Sugar, to taste

Combine espresso, rum, and cream. Chill. Pour into 6 tall glasses with ice. Fill glasses with ice cold sparkling water. Stir gently and sweeten with sugar to taste.

Serves six.

Grasshopper Espresso

Forget grasshopper pie—serve this exciting alternative instead.

1/4 cup (2 ounces) Vodka
1/4 cup (2 ounces) White Creme de
   Menthe
1 1/4 cup (10 ounces) brewed espresso,
   refrigerated
1 tablespoon heavy cream
Crushed ice

Mix ingredients in a blender or shaker, strain, and pour into cold cocktail glasses.

Serves two.

The Big Chill Espresso

1/8 cup (1 ounce) dark rum
1/8 cup (1 ounce) Kahlua
1/2 cup (4 ounces) brewed espresso,
  refrigerated
1/8 cup (1 ounce) heavy cream
1/2 teaspoon sugar
1/2 cup cracked ice
1 scoop vanilla ice cream

Shake all ingredients except the ice cream. Strain into a tall glass or 12 ounce goblet and top with ice cream. Serve with straws and a long-handled spoon.

Serves one.

The Jumpy Monkey

Don't knock it until you've tried it. The concoction won't have you swinging from a tree, but it might put you in the mood to "monkey around."

1/2 cup (4 ounces) brewed espresso, at
   room temperature
1/2 cup (4 ounces) cream of coconut
1 ripe banana
2 scoops vanilla ice cream
1/4 cup (2 ounces) rum (preferably dark
   rum)
8 to 10 ice cubes, shredded
2 tablespoons coconut, sweetened
Nutmeg, to garnish

Into a blender put the espresso, cream of coconut, banana, ice cream, rum, and ice cubes. Blend at high speed until liquified. Pour into two tall glasses that have been frosted in the freezer for a half hour or so. Top with grated coconut and sprinkle with nutmeg to garnish.

Serves two.

Bourbon Street Punch

1 quart bourbon
6 cups (48 ounces) brewed espresso, at
  room temperature
1 pint half-and-half
1/2 cup (4 ounces) Amaretto
1 quart ice cream, vanilla or coffee, half
  thawed
Chocolate shavings, optional

In a large pitcher, combine bourbon, espresso, half-and-half, and Amaretto. Chill well. Place the ice cream in a large punch bowl and slowly stir in the mixture from the pitcher. Decorate with chocolate shavings, if desired.

Serves thirty to thirty-five.

Espresso Fruit Punch

Just the right punch for all your cocktail parties.

1 fifth light or dark rum
1/2 cup lemon juice
1/4 cup sugar
1 cup (8 ounces) cranberry juice
1 cup (8 ounces) orange juice
1 cup (8 ounces) strong tea
1 cup (8 ounces) brewed espresso, at
   room temperature
1 dozen cloves
Thin lemon slices to garnish

Mix ingredients in a punch bowl and add ice cubes or ice block. Garnish with thin lemon slices.

Serves twenty.

Espresso Kahlua

❖◆❖

Kahlua is made with instant coffee. This uses freshly brewed espresso instead. An intense variation of Kahlua, this makes a wonderful base for a variety of drinks. Our personal favorite is an Espresso Kahlua White Russian (kahlua, vodka, half-and-half on ice). This variation comes to us from Teri Hope of the Los Gatos, California, Coffee Roasting Company.

3 cups brown sugar
2 cups (16 ounces) brewed espresso, hot
2 tablespoons pure vanilla extract
2 vanilla beans (split in half lengthwise)
1 quart brandy

Dissolve the brown sugar in the hot espresso. Let cool and add the vanilla extract. Refrigerate. Add the brandy, blending thoroughly. Pour the mixture into dark-tinted quart-size bottles, adding 1 split vanilla bean to each bottle. Let stand for a minimum of 30 days in a dark, cool spot. You may transfer kahlua into smaller bottles at this time if you wish.

Yields two quarts liqueur.

3
Savory Sauces and Entrees

Java Barbecue Sauce

◆◆

This is one of our favorite recipes for a lazy afternoon barbecue with good friends. We like it best as a glaze for chicken, lamb, or pork. Our friends have since told us that they use the recipe as a base but add or subtract to the ingredients as the mood fits.

3 tablespoons olive oil
1/2 cup finely chopped onion
1/2 cup (4 ounces) brewed espresso, hot
 or cold
1 cup ketchup or cocktail sauce
1 tablespoon lemon juice
1 tablespoon worcestershire sauce
3 tablespoons brown sugar
1/2 tablespoon dry mustard
1/4 teaspoon garlic powder/salt
2 tablespoons honey

In a saucepan, heat the olive oil. Add the onion and saute until transparent, about 3 minutes. Add the remaining ingredients and heat until blended and hot, stirring occasionally. Cool to room temperature, then refrigerate. After the charcoal is lit, remove the sauce from the refrigerator and warm over medium heat. This yields enough sauce to coat/glaze one whole chicken, or 3 pounds of lamb or pork, cut in serving pieces.

Yields about two cups of sauce.

Espresso Jack Daniels Rib Sauce

This sauce will make you sit up and take notice. It's not for the timid. Also, try it with beef kabobs or steak.

1/2 cup (4 ounces) brewed espresso, at
    room temperature
1/2 cup (4 ounces)Jack Daniels bourbon
3 tablespoons olive oil
1/2 cup onion, minced fine
2 cloves garlic, minced fine
1/2 cup (4 ounces) tomato paste or
    ketchup
1 tablespoon lemon juice
2 tablespoons tabasco sauce
1/2 teaspoon ground cayenne pepper (or
    chili powder)
2 tablespoons worcestershire sauce
1 tablespoon dry mustard
2 tablespoons honey

Mix the espresso and Jack Daniels in a deep bowl. In a saucepan, saute the onion and garlic in the olive oil until light golden brown. Remove from the heat and stir in the remaining ingredients. Add more or less tabasco and cayenne according to your preferences. Thoroughly blend the ingredients from the saucepan with the espresso and Jack Daniels. This yields enough to coat 3 pounds of pork or beef spareribs.

We recommend marinating the ribs overnight in this sauce before barbecuing. Barbecue slowly over low heat and continue to baste with any excess until done. Remember, the slower the better in barbecue.

Yields about 2 cups sauce.

Pork Tenderloin with Espresso Sauce

❖◆

There's an added bonus with this recipe—a mouth-watering aroma all through the house. We call this carefree cooking. Once the sauce is on the roast—we know we're guaranteed a rich flavor.

1 1/2 to 2 pounds pork tenderloin
1 cup (8 ounces)brewed espresso, cold or
   hot
1/3 cup unsalted butter
2 teaspoons worcestershire sauce
1 1/2 teaspoons dry mustard
1 tablespoon lemon juice
1 teaspoon sugar
Tabasco sauce, to taste

Start roasting the pork at low temperature, 325°F. (Pork is more succulent this way.) Then prepare the sauce. Combine the remaining ingredients in a saucepan. Heat gently and stir until butter melts. Brush over the pork periodically while it roasts. Serve what's left in a sauceboat.

Yields one and one-half cups of sauce.

Espresso Spaghetti Sauce

We love this with angel hair or vermicelli—but you could use it for layering lasagna.

1 pound ground beef or ground pork
1 1/2 cups sliced fresh mushrooms
1/2 cup chopped onion
1/2 cup chopped green pepper
2 garlic cloves, minced
1 cup (8 ounces) brewed espresso, hot or cold
2 cans (14 1/2 ounces each) Italian stewed tomatoes
1 8-ounce can tomato sauce
1 bay leaf
1 teaspoon sugar
1/2 teaspoon salt
Basil, thyme, or oregano, to taste

In a Dutch oven, cook meat, mushrooms, onion, green pepper, and garlic until meat is brown. Drain fat from pan. Dab with paper towels to remove most of the grease. Stir in the remaining ingredients and bring to a boil. Reduce heat, cover, and simmer 30 minutes. Uncover and simmer 10 to 15 minutes more to desired consistency, stirring occasionally. Discard bay leaf. Serve over spaghetti with grated cheese on the side. This sauce tastes even better the next day.

Serves four.

Ham with Espresso Glaze

We love tradition, especially at holidays. But while an old-fashioned Thanksgiving or Christmas dinner just wouldn't be the same without a feast of homey favorites, we've gone ahead and surprised our guests with this wonderful glazed ham.

1 cup honey
1/2 (4 ounces) cup brewed espresso
1 teaspoon cinnamon
1/4 teaspoon ground cloves
1/4 cup packed brown sugar
1/2 cup dried apricots
1/2 cup maraschino cherries
6 to 8 pound smoked ham, uncooked
Parsley, for garnish

Combine all ingredients except the fruit and ham. Simmer for 15 minutes over very low heat. Put aside. Bake the ham in a slow oven (300°F), calculating 25 minutes per pound, until the meat thermometer registers 160°F. One hour before baking time is completed, remove from the oven. Remove rind of ham; score ham fat diagonally in both directions, making a diamond pattern. Skewer a dried apricot and a maraschino cherry on a toothpick and insert in a diamond. Repeat with remaining apricots and cherries. Return to the oven. Baste with espresso glaze at 15-minute intervals during the last hour of baking. Garnish with parsley.

Serves eight to twelve.

Traditional Southern Ham
with Red-Eye Gravy

◆◆◆

True Southerners, we rarely consider a weekend breakfast complete without a helping of ham and red-eye gravy. I guess you could say Mama taught us well.

3 slices country ham, sliced 1/8 inch thick
1/2 cup (4 ounces) brewed espresso, hot
or cold

Cut the ham slices in half and trim off the fat, reserving the trimmings. Cook the trimmings in a skillet until crisp, until about 2 tablespoons of drippings accumulate, then discard the trimmings. If necessary, add a bit of vegetable oil to the ham to produce 2 tablespoons in the skillet.

Cook the ham in the skillet in the hot drippings until it is browned on each side, about 10 minutes. Remove the ham to a warm platter and keep it warm.

Heat the skillet until it is very hot. Add the espresso quickly, taking care to avoid splattering. Bring the mixture to a boil, scraping the pan to remove the crusty bits. Continue cooking over high heat for 3 minutes, or until the mixture is reduced by half.

Pour the mixture into a bowl. Serve hot on the ham slices, grits, or biscuits.

Serves four.

Oven-Baked Espresso Spare Ribs

◆-◆

This recipe comes from Teri Hope, owner of the Los Gatos Coffee Roasting Company. Teri has gained a reputation as one of the premier West Coast roasters. She is a true innovator when it comes to using espresso in cooking.

1/2 cup finely chopped onion
2 tablespoons olive oil
1 cup (8 ounces) brewed espresso, hot or cold
1/2 cup molasses
1/2 cup lemon juice (not concentrate)
4 tablespoons mustard (Dijon style is recommended)
1 tablespoon worcestershire sauce
4 pounds pork or beef spareribs

Saute the onion in olive oil until soft. Add the remaining liquid ingredients and stir thoroughly to blend. Bring to a low boil and remove from heat. Allow the sauce to cool slightly and pour half of the sauce over the spareribs. Bake in a 350°F oven for 2 hours while basting with remaining sauce.

Serves four.

Espresso Special Chili

❖◆❖

This hardy dish lets you ease into quick, mid-week winter dinners with full flavor fare. It's great for football parties, too!

1 pound beef, coarsely ground
1 cup chopped onion
1/2 cup chopped pepper
1/2 cup chopped celery
2 cloves garlic, minced
1 can (16 ounces) stewed tomatoes
2 cans (16 ounces) red kidney beans
1 cup (8 ounces) brewed espresso, hot or
   cold
2 cans (10 1/2 ounces) beef broth
2 to 3 tablespoons chili powder
1/2 teaspoon dried basil, crushed
1/4 teaspoon cayenne pepper
1 cup shredded Cheddar cheese, optional

In a large saucepan, cook the ground beef, onion, green pepper, celery, and garlic until the meat is browned. Drain the fat. Stir in the undrained tomatoes, kidney beans, espresso, broth, tomato sauce, chili powder, basil, and pepper. Bring to a boil; reduce heat. Cover and simmer for 20 minutes. Serve in bowls topped with shredded Cheddar cheese, if desired.

Serves four.

Espresso Party Meatballs

When we serve these delectable miniature marvels at cocktail soirees, we always hear applause. These can be used as an hors d' oeuvre or entree.

1 pound ground pork or ground lamb
1 pound ground beef or ground veal
2 cloves garlic, crushed
1 onion, finely chopped
1/4 teaspoon dried savory
1/4 teaspoon pepper
1/4 teaspoon ground nutmeg
2 teaspoons salt
1 cup bread crumbs
1 tablespoon prepared mustard
1 dash tabasco sauce
2 teaspoons worcestershire sauce

1/2 cup flour
4 strips raw bacon, cut into small pieces
1 cup (8 ounces) brewed espresso, hot or cold
1/2 cup red wine, preferably Burgundy
1/4 cup water
Salt, to taste
1 1/2 tablespoons flour
1/4 cup cold water
1 cup sour cream, optional

In a bowl, combine all ingredients up to the flour. Mix well. It may be simplest to use your hands. Form the mixture into approximately 30 meatballs and dust them with flour.

Cook the bacon until crisp and brown and remove it from the pan. Saute the meatballs in the bacon drippings until lightly browned. Add the espresso, wine, and salt, and simmer for 15 minutes.

Return the bacon to the pan and stir gently. Make a smooth paste with the flour and 1/4 cup of cold water and stir it into the pan. Cook the mixture gently for 5 more minutes. Serve over noodles or rice, with a dollop of sour cream, if desired.

Serves six to eight.

Beef Bourguignonne

◆◆

This classic French stew is a masterpiece. Set the scene with French bread, a hearty cheese and a robust red wine from Provence or the Rhone. C'est magnifique!

1 pound lean salt pork, cut into 2-inch long, thin strips
1/2 cup cornmeal
4 tablespoons olive oil
3 cloves garlic, minced
1 cup chopped onion
1/2 cup chopped shallots (or onions)
3 pounds chuck roast, cut into 3/4-inch cubes
4 tablespoons flour
3 cups whole, medium-size fresh mushrooms
1 cup (8 ounces) Burgundy wine
1 cup (8 ounces) Cognac (any brand—save the good stuff for your snifter)
1 cup (8 ounces) brewed espresso, hot or cold
12 ounces beef bouillon (canned or home-made stock)
4 medium carrots, cut in 3/4-inch rounds
4 potatoes, skin on, chopped into bite-size pieces
2 tablespoons parsley, chopped fresh

Lightly dredge the salt pork strips in cornmeal. In a large Dutch oven, brown the salt pork strips in olive oil. Remove the strips when done and set aside. Saute the garlic, onions and shallots in the salt pork drippings

until translucent. Dust the beef cubes with flour and add. Continue to stir to avoid burning. When the beef is lightly browned, remove and drain the fat. Add the mushrooms, cooked salt pork, and liquids. Stir to blend. Bring to a low boil, reduce the heat, cover tightly, and simmer for 1/2 hour. Watch out for too much reduction of liquid. It should just cover the meat. You may have to add a little water or more beef bouillon. After 1/2 hour, add the carrots and potatoes and continue to simmer until the meat is tender, about another 1/2 hour. The carrots and potatoes should be cooked but slightly firm. Serve in bowls or on a plate over noodles or rice. Garnish with parsley.

Serves six.

Sausage Gumbo

This hearty dish is just the ticket to warm you up on a cold winter night. We recommend using a good Cajun-style sausage, spicy but not hot. Bruce Aidells makes a particularly good sausage of this type.

1 1/2 cups dry kidney beans (or 16 ounces canned)

3 cups water

1/2 cup chopped onion

3 cloves garlic, minced

1/4 pound lean salt pork, cut into thin strips

1 pound Cajun sausage, whole links cut in 1-inch rounds

1 bay leaf

1 cup (8 ounces) brewed espresso, hot or cold

1/2 pound okra, cut into bite-size pieces (fresh or frozen)

2 stalks celery, cut into 1/2-inch pieces

1 tablespoon File Gumbo (a Cajun-style spice blend, available in most grocery stores)

1 tablespoon tabasco sauce

1 1/2 cups white rice

2 cups water

Soak the kidney beans in water for 6 to 8 hours or overnight, changing the water once to clean the beans. When ready to use, drain and rinse. In a large Dutch oven, put the beans and 3 cups water (2 cups water if using canned), heat to a boil, then lower to simmer.

In a separate pan, saute the onion and garlic until lightly browned, add the sausage and salt pork, and continue sauteing until done (the sausage should be cooked throughout, the salt pork crisp and brown). Add the sauteed ingredients along with the bay leaf, espresso, okra, celery, file gumbo, and tabasco sauce to the beans. Stir to blend. Simmer on low heat for 1 hour. Check every 1/2 hour, stirring to avoid burning. Watch to see if the water has evaporated. Add 1/2 cup of water at a time if needed. If using canned kidney beans, reduce the time to 1/2 hour. After 1 hour (dried kidney beans) or 1/2 hour (canned), add the rice and 2 cups water. Stir to blend and continue to simmer for 1 hour or until the rice is cooked. The gumbo should be thick with most of the liquid absorbed. Serve in bowls with a crusty bread. Don't worry about leftovers; it tastes even better the second day.

Serves four to six.

New Orleans-Style Red Beans and Rice

❖◆❖

This recipe is a time-honored family heirloom. We love to share this "taste of Louisiana" with friends.

1 1/2 cups dried kidney beans (16 ounces, canned)
Water, to cover
3 cups water
1/2 cup chopped onion
2 cloves garlic, minced
2 tablespoons olive oil
1 bay leaf
1 cup (8 ounces) brewed espresso, hot or cold
3/4 teaspoon salt
1/2 teaspoon fennel seed, crushed
1/2 teaspoon ground red pepper, optional
1 1/2 cups white rice
1 cup water

Soak the kidney beans in water for 6 to 8 hours or overnight. Change the water once to clean the beans. When ready to use, drain and rinse. In a large saucepan, place the beans and 3 cups water and heat to a boil.

In a separate pan, saute the onion and garlic in the olive oil until lightly browned. Add the onion and garlic, along with the bay leaf, espresso, salt, fennel seed, and red pepper to the beans. Boil for 2 minutes, stirring to blend ingredients, then reduce the heat to simmer and cover tightly. Cook the beans for 2 hours (if you used dried beans), 20 minutes for canned. Add the rice and 1 cup water, cover, and simmer until the rice is done (about 20 minutes). Occasionally check and stir. If necessary, add a few tablespoons of water to keep

the dish moist. When done, the liquids should be absorbed by the beans and rice. Serve in bowls with a loaf of French bread or corn bread, or as a side dish with the rest of your meal.

Serves four to six.

New England Baked Beans—
Espresso Style

◆◆◆

We forget everyday doldrums with good friends and comfort foods. Baked beans are one of our favorites. We serve these at picnics, on summer camping excursions, after fall hikes, and during the World Series on television.

1/2 cup chopped onion
2 cans (1 pound each) Boston-style baked
  beans
1 teaspoon dry mustard
Salt and pepper, to taste
1/2 cup molasses
1/4 cup packed brown sugar
1/2 cup (4 ounces) brewed espresso
1/2 cup boiling water
1/4 pound lean salt pork, trimmed

Place the chopped onion and beans in a deep casserole dish. Mix the dry mustard with the beans and add salt and pepper to taste. Combine the molasses, brown sugar, espresso, and boiling water; pour over the beans. Score the salt pork with a sharp knife. Bury the salt pork in the beans. Bake in a moderate oven (350°F) for 1 hour, stirring occasionally.

Serves six.

4
Desserts and Dessert Sauces

Tiramisu

This treasured recipe comes to us from Abby Nash, owner-chef of Abby's Restaurant in Ithaca, New York. Tiramisu means pick-me-up or lift-me-up in Italian, reflecting the large amounts of uncooked liqueur and strong coffee in this dessert. While preparing tiramisu does not require an oven, it does need to be made a few hours ahead of serving time to allow the flavors to penetrate the ladyfingers. Abby recommends Bistefani brand Savoiardi (7-ounce package). Stella d' Oro Margherite may be used but, as they are heavier, a 14-ounce package will be needed and the espresso needs to be increased to 8 ounces.

1 package (7 ounces) ladyfingers
3/4 cup (6 ounces) brewed espresso, at
   room temperature

2 tablespoons marsala
2 tablespoons Amaretto
1/2 pound mascarpone
1 cup heavy cream
1/4 cup finely chopped or grated
   semisweet chocolate

Use a 8-by-11-inch glass pan. Mix the espresso, marsala, and Amaretto in a measuring cup.

In a large bowl, very lightly beat the mascarpone to smooth it out. Beat the cream until it holds soft peaks. Beat 1/4 cup of the cream into the mascarpone and gently fold in the rest. The mixture may be a bit lumpy but that's okay.

There will be 2 layers of each ingredient. Place half of the ladyfingers in the bottom of the pan, flat side down, and brush with half of the soaking liquid. Cover with half of the mascarpone and sprinkle with half of the chocolate. Repeat with rest of ingredients. Sprinkle the chocolate over the third and fifth layers of filling. Chill approximately 4 hours before cutting with a serrated knife.

Serves nine.

Amaretto Espresso Cake

If you're looking for a low-calorie dessert, this is the wrong recipe. If you want something sinfully delicious, then read on. We suggest you worry about calories later.

1 envelope unflavored gelatin
1 cup light cream
1 package (8-ounce) cream cheese, softened
1/3 cup sugar
1 cup (8 ounces) brewed espresso, refrigerated
1/4 cup (2 ounces) Amaretto
Powdered sugar
Semisweet chocolate, shaved

Lightly oil a bundt pan. In a small saucepan, sprinkle the gelatin over the cream. Let stand for 5 minutes to soften. Over low heat, heat until the gelatin is dissolved, stirring occasionally.

In a large mixing bowl, beat the cream cheese and sugar at medium speed until light and fluffy. Reduce the speed and gradually mix in the espresso, Amaretto, and gelatin mixture until well blended.

Pour into the bundt pan and cover with waxed paper. Refrigerate for at least 7 hours. Unmold onto a serving plate, sift the powdered sugar around the top, and garnish with shaved chocolate.

Serves six.

Louisiana Espresso Cake

❖❖

This is a fine combination of espresso and spices. It stays fresh, wrapped in wax paper, for several days.

1/2 cup butter, softened
1 cup sugar
2 eggs, well beaten
1/2 cup seeded raisins, chopped
1/4 cup molasses
1 teaspoon cinnamon
1 teaspoon mace
1 teaspoon cloves
1 teaspoon baking soda
1/2 cup (4 ounces) brewed espresso,
  refrigerated
2 cups flour, sifted

Cream the butter well and add the sugar slowly. In another bowl, mix the eggs, raisins, molasses, and spices. Stir into the butter and sugar mixture.

Dissolve the baking soda in the espresso and stir into the above mixture. Mix well.

Add the flour, folding in gently. Bake in a greased 9-inch square pan in a preheated 350°F oven for about 40 minutes. Cut into squares and serve either warm or cold with cappuccino.

Serves eight.

Espresso Chocolate Cheesecake

This is a very rich, dense dessert. Your choice of chocolate will certainly affect the outcome. The chocolate made by the Belgian company, Callebaut, is quite good.

1 cup chocolate cookie crumbs
1/2 cup butter, unsalted, melted, divided
1 cup granulated sugar
4 eggs, large
1 1/2 pounds cream cheese, softened
1 pound semisweet chocolate
1 teaspoon vanilla extract
2 tablespoons cocoa
2 1/2 cups sour cream, at room
  temperature
1/2 cup brewed espresso, refrigerated
1 cup shaved white chocolate

Crush the chocolate cookies and blend with 1/4 cup melted butter. Press the mixture into the bottom of a 10-inch spring-form pan and chill for 1 hour. Preheat the oven to 425°F. In a large bowl, beat the sugar and eggs until light and fluffy. (If using an electric mixer, use the medium speed setting.) Add the softened cream cheese gradually while beating. In a double boiler, melt the chocolate in the top half. Allow the chocolate to cool slightly before adding it to the cream cheese mixture. Slowly beat the mixture, adding the remaining 1/4 cup melted butter, vanilla, cocoa, sour cream, and espresso. Pour the batter on the chilled crust. Place the spring-form pan on a cookie sheet and bake for 1 hour. The center will be soft.

Let the cheesecake cool while on a wire rack, cover with aluminum foil, and refrigerate overnight. Remove the sides of the springform. Garnish the top of the cheesecake with the shaved white chocolate.

Serves sixteen to twenty-four.

Espresso Coffee Cake

◆◆◆

3 eggs
2/3 cup sugar
1/2 cup butter, softened
2/3 cup flour, sifted
1 tablespoon baking powder
2 cups (16 ounces) brewed espresso, at
room temperature

Filling
1/2 cup butter, softened
3 tablespoons confectioner's sugar
2 tablespoons brewed espresso, at room
temperature

Beat eggs well. Add the sugar and butter. Beat well. Stir in the flour and baking powder until smooth. Add the espresso very slowly. Turn the mixture into a greased, round cake tin and bake in a preheated oven at 350°F, until a toothpick inserted into the center comes out clean. Put on a rack to cool.

Make the filling in an electric mixer or by hand. Combine the butter and confectioner's sugar until light and creamy. Add the espresso slowly. Cut the cake horizontally into 2 halves, spread the filling, and put the cake back together.

Serves four to six.

Espresso Kuchen

❖◆❖

We love these on Christmas day.

3 cups flour, sifted
3 teaspoons baking powder
Dash salt
2 cups brown sugar, firmly packed
1/2 cup shortening
1/2 cup butter
1/2 cup (4 ounces) brewed espresso, at
   room temperature
1/2 cup evaporated milk
1/8 teaspoon baking soda
2 eggs, beaten well
1 teaspoon ground cinnamon

Preheat the oven to 375°F. Mix the flour, baking powder, salt, and brown sugar together. Cut in the shortening and butter, using 2 knives or a pastry blender. Measure out 1 cup of this mixture and set aside for the topping. Keep the remainder in a bowl.

In another bowl, combine the espresso, evaporated milk, and baking soda. Add this to the flour mixture in the bowl and mix well. Add the eggs and blend. Spoon the batter into a greased muffin tin filling each depression half full. Add the cinnamon to the reserved topping mixture and sprinkle on top of each muffin. Bake for 25 minutes.

Yields one dozen.

Espresso Pecan Pie

What Southern meal would be complete without pecan pie? Come to our house and you'll be served vanilla ice cream on the side.

3 eggs, beaten
3/4 cup molasses
3/4 cup light corn syrup
1/2 cup (4 ounces) brewed espresso, at
   room temperature
2 tablespoons butter, melted
1/4 teaspoon salt
1 teaspoon vanilla
1 cup chopped pecan meats
4 tablespoons flour
1 (8-inch) unbaked pie shell
1 cup heavy cream, whipped, optional

Preheat the oven to 375°F. Combine the eggs, molasses, corn syrup, espresso, melted butter, salt, and vanilla. Mix thoroughly. Combine the pecans and flour, add to the liquid mixture, and pour into the unbaked pie shell. Bake 40 to 45 minutes in a moderate oven (375°F) or until firm. Cool before cutting. Garnish with whipped cream, if desired. Portions should be small because of the richness of the pie.

Serves eight.

Espresso Walnut Ginger Crumb Crust

We found this pie crust is wonderful for both pies and puddings. Bake a couple of them, freeze, and save for on-the-spot desserts.

1/2 cup ground walnut meats
3/4 cup crushed gingersnap crumbs
2 tablespoons sugar
1/4 cup butter, melted
1/2 cup (4 ounces) brewed espresso, at room temperature

Mix together all ingredients. Press firmly into a 9-inch pie pan to form a crust. Bake in a moderate oven (350°F) for 8 minutes. Cool.

Yields one pie crust.

Mocha Fudge Espresso

◆◇◆

Southerners love fudge. We admit it. Since we also love espresso—why not combine the fudge and espresso?

1 tablespoon butter
2 squares baking chocolate
1/4 teaspoon salt
1 pound sifted confectioner's sugar
1/4 cup (2 ounces) brewed espresso, hot

Place the butter, chocolate, and salt in the top of a double boiler. Heat. When melted, stir until well blended. Remove the double boiler from the heat but keep the top pan over hot water. Stir in the sugar and espresso alternately, beating after each addition. As soon as the mixture is well blended, pour into a greased 8-inch square pan. Cool and cut in squares.

Yields eighteen to twenty squares.

Espresso Trifle

◆◆

Trifles are surefire hits. We make this recipe time and again because it's aesthetically pleasing and tastes fabulous.

2 egg whites
1/2 pound confectioner's sugar
1/2 pound butter, melted
1/2 cup (4 ounces) brewed espresso, refrigerated
1/2 cup (4 ounces) brandy
10 ounces ladyfingers (There are many brands available at your local grocers; we recommend Bistefani brand Savoiardi or Stella d'Oro Margherite.)
4 ounces semisweet chocolate, shaved
1 cup heavy cream, whipped, optional

Beat the egg whites until stiff. Fold in the sugar and butter to form a creamy mixture. Separately, soak the ladyfingers for 10 minutes in the espresso mixed with brandy. In a glass dish or bowl, alternate layers of ladyfingers topped with the creamy mixture and shaved chocolate until all the ingredients are used up. Chill for 1 hour. Garnish with whipped cream if desired.

Serves six.

Mocha Espresso Balls

Following dinner, we often serve dessert buffet-style. This recipe is perfect for a buffet. We place the mocha espresso balls on a tray so our guests can help themselves in a leisurely fashion. Be warned—you will be asked to fill the tray again, again, and again!

1 large (7-ounce) box vanilla wafers
2 cups confectioner's sugar
1 cup finely chopped pecans
2 tablespoons cocoa, unsweetened
1/4 cup heavy cream
1/4 cup (2 ounces) brewed espresso, at
   room temperature

Crush the vanilla wafers into fine crumbs (there should be 2 cups). Add the sugar; mix well. Stir in the pecans and cocoa. Add the cream and espresso. Mix well; shape into balls about 3/4 inch in diameter. Roll some of the balls in additional confectioner's sugar. Chill. (Do not bake.)

Yields about four dozen.

Espresso/Brandy Cookies

This is a Christmas-time favorite in our house. Next time, leave some for Santa. They'll be gone by morning. Ho, ho, ho!

1/2 cup butter
3/4 cup sugar
2 eggs, beaten
1/4 cup (2 ounces) brewed espresso, at
   room temperature
1/4 cup (2 ounces) brandy
1 1/2 cups sifted flour
1 1/2 teaspoons baking powder
1/4 teaspoon salt
2 cups wheat flakes, like Wheaties

Cream the butter and sugar. Add the well-beaten eggs and mix thoroughly. Stir in the espresso and brandy. Mix and sift the flour, baking powder and salt; add, and stir until smooth. Crush the wheat flakes slightly with a rolling pin, and roll a teaspoonful of the cookie mixture in the flakes. Place on a greased cookie sheet, 2 inches apart. Bake in a hot oven (400°F) for 12 minutes.

Yields about three dozen cookies.

Chocolate-Espresso Gelato

❖❖❖

This gelato is equivalent of a frozen mousse. You can add blanched and roasted hazelnuts and substitute Fra Angelico for the coffee liqueur. This recipe comes from Jim Tarantino, author of "Sorbets."

2 cups half-and-half
1/4 cup coarsely ground espresso beans
1/4 cup sugar
4 large egg yolks
1 teaspoon vanilla extract
Pinch of salt
2 teaspoons instant espresso*
6 ounces extra bittersweet chocolate
  broken into 1/2-inch pieces
3 tablespoons of coffee liqueur

In a medium-size saucepan, scald the half-and-half with the espresso beans until the cream turns a light brown. In a medium-size mixing bowl, combine the sugar, egg yolks, vanilla, and sugar. Strain the half-and-half and slowly whisk into the egg mixture; return the custard to the saucepan. Add the instant espresso and stir constantly over medium heat until the custard coats the back of a spoon, about 5 minutes. Do not boil. Remove from heat, add the chocolate, and stir until melted. Stir in the liqueur. Strain and cool. Freeze in your ice cream maker.

Yields eight servings.

* Instant espresso is used in this recipe as it adds concentrated flavor without adding extra liquid which would affect the texture and taste of the gelato.

Espresso Granita

◆◇◆

Anyone who likes espresso will love this ice. For added flavor, you can pour a tablespoon of Sambucca over each individual serving. This recipe comes to us from Jim Tarantino, author of "Sorbets."

1 lemon
1 1/2 cups (12 ounces) brewed espresso, hot
1 cup (8 ounces) good quality freshly brewed coffee, hot
1 cup water
1/3 cup sugar
Julienned lemon peel to garnish
6 tablespoons San Bucca (optional)

Wash the lemon and peel. Make sure the white pith is removed or the ice will be bitter. Combine the espresso and the regular coffee, add the lemon peel, and steep for about 20 minutes. Strain the espresso/coffee to remove the peel.

Make a syrup by combining the water and sugar in a saucepan and bring to a boil. Simmer for 5 minutes. Remove the syrup from the heat and cool.

Juice the lemon and combine with the coffee and syrup. Pour into a 9-inch by 13-inch by 2-inch cake pan and cover with plastic wrap. Freeze until the mixture is set, about 4 hours.

To serve, scrape the granita with a spoon or fork to create small shavings and spoon into individual chilled dessert bowls. Garnish with the julienned lemon peel.

Serves six.

Espresso Russian Cream

Yet another innovative dish from Teri Hope.

1/2 cup granulated sugar
1/2 pint half-and-half
1 envelope gelatin
1/2 cup (4 ounces) brewed espresso, refrigerated
1 pint sour cream
1 teaspoon pure vanilla extract
1/4 cup unsalted pistachios or slivered, raw almonds

In the top of a double boiler, warm the sugar and half-and-half. Combine with the gelatin and espresso, stirring thoroughly to dissolve the gelatin. Do not boil. Remove from the heat and add the sour cream and vanilla extract. Stir until smooth, chill thoroughly, and spoon into parfait glasses. Top with pistachios or almonds.

Serves six.

Mocha Espresso Pudding

3/4 cup sugar
1 cup sifted flour
2 teaspoons baking powder
1/8 teaspoon salt
1 teaspoon cinnamon
1/2 teaspoon allspice
1/8 teaspoon cloves
1/2 teaspoon nutmeg
3 tablespoons butter, melted
1/2 cup milk
1 teaspoon vanilla
1/2 cup brown sugar
1/2 cup sugar
4 tablespoons cocoa
1 cup (8 ounces) brewed espresso,
  refrigerated
1 cup heavy cream, whipped, optional
1 pint coffee ice cream, optional

Mix and sift 3/4 cup sugar, flour, baking powder, salt, and spices. Add the melted butter; mix well. Combine the milk and vanilla, add, and mix well. Pour into 8-inch greased square cake pan. Combine the brown sugar, 1/2 cup sugar and cocoa; sprinkle evenly over the batter. Pour the cold espresso over the surface. Bake in a moderate oven (305°F) for 40 to 50 minutes. Serve warm with whipped cream or coffee ice cream, or both.

Yields approximately eighteen to twenty squares.

Frozen Chocolate Cappuccino Mousse

This dessert recipe is more than an indulgence for chocolate lovers—it's heaven. Believe us, we know.

3/4 cup (6 ounces) brewed espresso, hot
1/2 cup sugar
4 large egg yolks
1/4 cup (2 ounces) Kahlua
1/2 tablespoon cinnamon
1 quart chocolate ice cream, softened
2 cups heavy cream, whipped

In a saucepan over medium heat, boil the espresso and sugar for 4 minutes.

Place the egg yolks in a small mixing bowl, and at medium speed, beat in the hot espresso/sugar mixture in a thin stream. Continue beating until the yolks are thick and pale colored, about 3 minutes. Stir in the Kahlua and cinnamon. Pour into a larger mixing bowl and fold in the whipped cream.

Divide the mixture into 2 loaf pans. Randomly spoon the ice cream on the mousse mixture, cover with plastic wrap, and freeze until firm, at least 7 hours. Spoon into goblets, top with additional whipped cream, and serve with plenty of gourmet cookies.

Serves six.

Espresso-Scotch Frosting

❖◆❖

If you ever need a subtle change for a basic recipe, think espresso.

1/4 cup butter
1/2 cup brown sugar
1/4 cup (2 ounces) brewed espresso, at
**   room temperature**
1/4 cup (2 ounces) Scotch whiskey
3 cups confectioner's sugar

Cream the butter. Add the brown sugar and continue creaming until smooth. Mix the whiskey and espresso in a cup. Add the confectioner's sugar to the creamed mixture alternately with the whiskey and espresso liquid. Use as a filling between split layers of a 7-inch baker's sponge cake and as frosting for outside a bundt cake.

Yields eight to twelve.

Maple Espresso Pancake/Waffle Topping

We call this the back-to-bed breakfast elixir. You will find that the sofa starts calling you for a nap as soon as you push away from this weekend breakfast. By the way, this sauce is also excellent on vanilla pudding or ice cream.

1 cup maple syrup
1/2 cup (8 ounces) brewed espresso, hot
3 tablespoons butter
1/2 cup chopped pecans, walnuts, etc.
1/4 cup finely chopped and peeled apples

Bring the maple syrup to a slow boil. Add the espresso and simmer for 3 more minutes, stirring constantly. Remove from the heat. Stir in the butter, nuts, and apples. Serve warm on your favorite pancakes or waffles.

Yields about 3 cups of syrup.

Mocha Rum Sauce

◆◆

Picture Sunday morning—breakfast in bed, the New York Times, someone you love. This and the following two sauces are not only tasty, but are quick and easy to prepare. They're great for topping your morning oatmeal, pancakes, or waffles. We usually save some as a delectable topping for vanilla ice cream late in the day.

1 package chocolate rum wafers
1/2 cup (4 ounces) brewed espresso, hot

Melt a package of wafers over hot water; add the espresso slowly, stirring until smooth. This sauce can be served hot or cold.

Yields one generous scoop of sauce.

Coffee Cream Sauce

This is particularly good over chocolate ice cream.

1/4 cup sugar
1/4 cup (2 ounces) brewed espresso
1/2 pint heavy cream, whipped

Stir the sugar in a heavy pan over low heat until it forms a golden-brown syrup. Remove from the heat. Gradually add the espresso. Return to the heat and boil until smooth. Cool slightly and fold into the whipped cream.

Yields one and one-half cups of sauce.

Coffee Rum Sauce

This sauce is best over vanilla ice cream. Better yet, fry some chopped walnuts in butter and sprinkle over the top of each serving.

1 cup sugar
1 1/2 cups (12 ounces) brewed espresso, hot
2 tablespoons cornstarch
3 tablespoons espresso, refrigerated
2 tablespoons butter
2 teaspoons dark rum, to taste

Melt the sugar slowly in a heavy skillet, stirring often. Add the espresso slowly, stirring constantly. Blend the cornstarch and cold espresso; stir in. Continue to cook and stir until the sauce boils and thickens. Remove from the heat. Add the butter and dark rum; stir until the butter dissolves.

Yields two cups.

Espresso Truffles

Richard Donnelly of Santa Cruz, California, one of the up and coming chocolatiers in the U.S., has offered to divulge his recipe for Espresso Truffles.

This recipe might seem like a lot of effort but its really worth the "truffle."

By European standards chocolate labeled "couverture" must have, by law, a minimum of 32% cocoa butter. This factor in chocolate will yield the best tasting results. Should you use another type of chocolate, the resulting texture and flavor will vary. You can find chocolate couverture at many gourmet shops. Callebaut and Valhrona both make fine couvertures. If you cannot find couverture, use semi-sweet or bitter-sweet dark chocolate.

1/2 pint heavy cream
1 1/4 pounds dark chocolate couverture
1/8 pound unsalted butter, softened
1/2 cup (4 ounces) brewed espresso

Coating
1 pound dark chocolate couverture, melted
1 cup powdered sugar
2 cups unsweetened cocoa powder

Finely chop the 1 1/4 pounds of chocolate and place in a deep bowl. Bring the heavy cream to a boil and immediately pour over the chopped chocolate. Stir slowly with a whisk until all the chocolate is melted and evenly mixed. Add the butter and espresso and whisk until thoroughly blended. Let the filling sit until soft and smooth. When it is firm enough to hold shape and yet soft enough to be easily shaped, with a pastry bag or teaspoon shape the filling into bite-size chocolate dumplings (about 1" diameter). Let set until firm. Dip your hands in powdered sugar (this will be repeated many times) and roll the pieces into balls and let set for several minutes. Ideally the mixture should be about 90 degrees—any hotter and the chocolate cannot hold its form.

Coating the truffles: Melt 1 pound of chocolate in a double boiler and allow it to cool to 90 degrees. Coat a sheet pan with cocoa powder. Dip your hands in the melted chocolate and roll each ball in your palm until coated with melted chocolate. Place each piece on the sheet pan. In order to coat with cocoa powder evenly before the chocolate sets, after you have coated each dozen, flip each truffle over with a fork until coated with cocoa powder. Repeat until all pieces are coated. Transfer truffles to a serving tray.

Store in a covered container out of direct sunlight. To refrigerate, store in a dry, tightly sealed container. When ready to use, bring the container back to room temperature with the lid still sealed (to avoid condensation from forming on the truffles).

Yields ninety truffles.

Reference Guide

We are confessed java junkies. No matter what part of the country (or the world) our travels take us, we automatically order espresso—in every restaurant, cafe, and hotel we stumble upon.

We read books on coffee the way others read novels, and we know exactly which day of the week the Food section will appear in the many newspapers we subscribe to. Scanning a magazine's table of contents is a hobby, too, in search of our favorite topic.

All the references we've included have been helpful to us in our understanding and appreciation of coffee and particularly espresso. We hope they will be a worthy addition to your library, too.

Jacki Baxter, *The Coffee Book*. Chartwell Books, Inc., Secaucus, New Jersey, 1985.

CBC, *Coffee Workshop Manual*. Coffee Brewing Ctr. of the Pan Amer. Coffee Bur., NY, NY, 1974.

Kenneth Davids, *Coffee: A Guide to Buying, Brewing and Enjoying*. 101 Productions, San Ramon, California, 1987.

Francesco and Riccardo Illy, *From Coffee to Espresso*. Officine Grafiche Mondadori, Verona, Italy, 1990.

Heinrich Eduard Jacob, *Coffee: The Epic of a Commodity*. The Viking Press, NY, NY, 1935.

Bernard Rothfos, *Coffee Consumption*. Gordian-Max Rieck GmbH, Hamburg, Germany, 1986.

Charles and Violet Schafer, *Coffee*. Yerba Buena Press, San Francisco, California, 1976.

Michael Sivetz, *Coffee Quality*. Sivetz Coffee, Inc., Corvallis, Oregon, Rev. 1990.

Joel, David, and Karl Schapira, *The Book of Coffee and Tea*. The New Amer. Library, NY, NY, 1982.

Peter Quimme, *The Signet Book of Coffee and Tea*. The New American Library, NY, NY, 1976.

Index

W

The Crossing Press
publishes a full line of cookbooks.
For a free catalog, call toll-free
800/777-1048